SELF WORTH

TABLE OF CONTENTS

INTRODUCTION

Self Worth is a term used to define a person's overall emotional evaluation of their worth. It is a judgment of oneself and an attitude toward the self. Self Worth encompasses beliefs such as 'I am competent,' 'I am worthy,' and emotions like triumph, despair, pride, and shame. People with healthy Self Worth like themselves and value their achievements. While every one lacks confidence on occasions people with low Self Worth feel unhappy or unsatisfied with themselves most of the time. In essence, how you see your Self Worth is your opinion of yourself. It can also refer to the state of mind where a person pushes their boundaries and encourages belief within oneself. It is something that comes from self-love. To have confidence in yourself, one must love oneself to get freedom from constant doubt.

CHAPTER 1

SELF WORTH: THE KEY TO SUCCESS

It won't be far-fetched to say that self-worth is the key to success. If not, it is the first step toward success. When a person has self-worth, they are halfway through their battle. People in school and workplaces achieve success by taking more initiative and being more forward and active in life. Moreover, they tend to make better decisions because of having confidence in themselves.

Thus, it makes them stand out from the crowd. When you stand apart, people will notice you. Therefore, it increases your chances of attaining success in life. Alternatively, if a person does not trust or believe in himself, it will be tough. They will find it hard to succeed because they will be exposed to failure and criticism. Thus, without self-worth, they may not get back on their feet as fast as someone with self-confidence.

In addition to gaining success, one also enjoys a variety of perks. For instance, you can find a job more efficiently.

Similarly, you may find the magnitude of a difficult job lesser than it is.

Importance Of Self-Worth

Self-worth allows us to face our failure and own up to it in a positive light. Moreover, it helps us to raise many times. This helps instill a quality that ensures we do not give up until we succeed.

Similarly, self-worth instills optimism in us. People who have self-confidence are not lucky, and they are brilliant. They do not rely on others to achieve success; they rely on their abilities.

While self-worth is essential, it is also important not to become overconfident. As we know, anything in excess can be wrong for us. Similarly, overconfidence is also no exception.

When you become overconfident, you do not acknowledge the criticism. When you don't do that, you do not work on yourself. Thus, it stops your growth. Overlooking all this will prove to be harmful.

So it is essential to have moderation which can let you attain just the right amount of self-worth and self-love, which will assure you success and happiness.

There are many words to describe how we feel about ourselves, think about ourselves, and act toward ourselves. It's understandable if they all start to blend for you; however, they are different concepts with unique meanings, findings, and purposes.

Do you feel you do not matter much and have little to offer? What's the point you ask yourself of making an effort? "Whatever I say won't make much difference, and I won't be noticed." These are signs of low self-worth. Such a way of seeing oneself can lead to a depressive mood.

There are several ways in which people value themselves and assess their self-worth.

Comparison With Others And Self-Worth

The common thing is to look for some way you are better than others. Perhaps you have a more competent car, a more extensive garden, or fashionable clothes. Or maybe you are socially popular or well-known for what you do at work. The Western world values winners - being more physically attractive, educationally advanced, or financially successful. But not everyone can beat the competition. There is always someone more affluent, better thought of, or influential than you or I. We can't all be at the top of the pile. And measuring oneself against others means that your sense of self-worth

will rise and fall in step with your latest success or failure. Research at the University of Michigan found that the students who reported more stress, anger, academic problems, and relationship conflicts based their self-worth on comparison with others on external things such as academic performance, physical appearance, and being socially approved. Self-appreciation and a sense of one's unique strengths and qualities mattered for a sense of selfworth. Some of these may not be valued by others. So how can one appreciate oneself when few do?

Doing Meaningful Things And Self-Worth

What is meaningful in life varies according to individual interests and experience, but doing something that you happen to value can help with self-worth. Studies are finding that helping others and volunteering positively affect how people feel about themselves.

Doing things for only external reasons can be demoralizing when the rewards don't come; a bonus from the company, or tip from a customer that didn't materialize, or the unforthcoming offer of employment from someone you are trying to impress. However, the worker who values getting a job done well and on time feels good about him- or herself even when the client or boss fails to show any thanks or praise. Everyone needs a few thanks from time to time. Being appreciated is what can keep us going. But when you depend upon it, you perhaps need to think again about what you set store by in what you do; what is essential about your input.

Adding Value To A Situation And Self-Worth

What seems to matter to self-worth is the attitude one brings to everyday activities and relationships - not just at work but in the home and community. If you attach importance to generosity, how generous is your attitude to those who need a little of your time? If you value patience in life, how patient are you with children? If you love home life, how supportive are you of your family? I would suggest that the more your ways of living are in harmony with the values you cherish, the more self-worth you will feel.

Unique Contribution And Self-Worth

Every person you meet can walk away from you, feeling just a little happier. This can be because of the way you deal with them, the effort you put in, and the interest you have shown. Feeling their appreciation if you get it is part of the delight. To my way of thinking, it doesn't matter in what circumstance you find yourself - at home, work, or play - there will always be an opportunity to add value to the situation by what you choose to say and do. What this is will vary according to who you are - not only your values but your strengths, experience, and disposition, for everyone brings something slightly different and unique to the table. No two people have the same way of being useful where there is a need. It might be a thoughtful suggestion, a warmth of concern, a sense of humor, appropriate knowledge, relevant personal experience, practical action, sensitive empathy, and wise insight. The list could go on.

Spiritual Teachings And Self-Worth

Feeling good about what you do is very different from feeling you are good. A spiritual perspective acknowledges some higher power beyond that of human beings. According to this view, all people who behave well, whatever their race, education, and background, are united because there is an infinite creative force behind all that is humane in the world. All the worthwhile things we do result from being a willing channel for this higher power. I am not good, but I can feel good because the more I put myself into a situation, the more I will get out of it as I experience the inflow of energy

Fulfillment, And Enlightenment.

Similarly, spiritual philosopher Emanuel Swedenborg had an all-embracing concept of a Divine Source. He also wrote about the image of what we might call 'a universal human'. This visionary picture of a healthy, well-formed human being consists of a myriad of people who did good things that have ever existed. All these live in an afterlife of heaven. Each is said to be uniquely different, but each fits into the whole as an essential bit so that the whole body works. In other words, every human soul has been created to become a particular part of the all. Everyone can be important in their way.

Each of us can choose to remain separate and self-orientated or instead choose to serve some unique function by doing something good that adds to the healthy functioning of society.

CHAPTER 2

USING YOUR PURPOSE TO FUEL YOUR SELF-WORTH AND VISA-VERSA

A sense of 'self-worth' and a sense of 'purpose' arc crucial ingredients that contribute substantially to our overall wellbeing; the neglect of these critical components can lead us to a place of emotional bankruptcy, and when we arrive at such a low ebb, recovery can be a long painful process. Prevention is always better than cure, so while we have our wits about us, let's examine these two components and discover techniques for installing them into our hardware in such a way as to enhance the operation of our internal engine. I've observed in my own life that it's complicated to maintain a strong sense of self-worth if I don't have clarity about my life's purpose. I'm talking here on an emotional level. This is probably because aimlessness and the sense that all my efforts and endeavors have no real significance are incredibly demoralizing. When in life you deem most of the activities you're involved in demoralizing, it'll not be easy to feel particularly valuable.

So here, we've identified an emotional cycle that operates externally but leaves an internal residue, which, if we ignore it, has the potential for destructive consequences. I'll throw you a couple of tools to help restore and maintain these critical building blocks, so you can operate optimally and live a purposeful existence that reflects the Creator and fulfills the drives and impulses intrinsic to your wiring. Living out your purpose is the road to destiny and is foundational to a life of fulfillment.

Purpose

The feeling that what we occupy ourselves with daily is linked to our fundamental life purpose is both energizing and rewarding. A necessary pre-requisite, though, is to know what our life purpose is. Stopping and considering this with pen and paper is a precious exercise. I would recommend mind mapping your thoughts to assess the various components of your life purpose. The more honest you can be in genuinely assessing yourself will enable you to know what contributes to and subtracts from your sense of purpose. Having done the necessary self-examination and taking practical steps to build your life around the values, you have uncovered the next course of action to undertake.

This may not be as easy as all that, perhaps because of your current economic circumstance or other factors that you may need to consider. Purpose itself is a driving force; it comes from knowing you personal 'why' and cultivating your vision as a source of inspiration and motivation. Each individual's life purpose has inherent differences; drawing inspiration from the lives of others who are doing what we aspire to do to cultivate our dreams can be very useful. But the comparison is almost always discouraging. Nobody else can make your journey, and the lives your life will affect will be different from those of someone else.

Self-Worth

Unfortunately, we don't have a lot of say in the early cultivation of our intrinsic sense of self-worth. I dare say the early years contribute the lion's share of self-worth we bring to the table until we do something about our self-worth and invest in its cultivation because we detect holes in this critical part of our armor. When for years you have, say, working in a field that never taps your specific gifts, and you don't have any other outlet for them, your self-worth will begin to leek. When we fail in areas of our lives that we deem essential, our self-worth will grow leek inevitably, or when we surround ourselves with people who are negative, unsupportive, or lacking in vision and unable to recognize our potential or worth, our self-worth begins to leek. And an empty self-worth tank is a recipe for depression, hopelessness, self-pity, and even suicide. It doesn't necessarily have to be so obviously drastic; a low sense of self-worth will prevent us from fulfilling our potential or from using our innate gifts to rise above many of life's obstacles and circumstances. We must examine the condition of our self-worth if we desire to cultivate a better life for ourselves, those who depend upon us, or others whose lives will inevitably be touched by a purposeful cultivated existence, that's maximizing itself because it believes in itself.

Recently, I had to examine what at the core of my being was lacking and in need of fundamental cultivation. I realized that numerous destructive tendencies, unwanted habits, and negative behaviors could be traced to a lack of self-worth and purpose. I'm a great believer in getting to the core of the matter rather than faffing with the peripheral garbage that, unfortunately, often has to be waded through to discover the cause of our issues. When I recognized these issues at a core level, I got excited about finding a solution. I think it's safe to say that most of us want to live a purposeful life and that to wade in the troughs of low self-worth for a lifetime is certainly not our ideal picture of optimal living. So first, I recommend we do an all-out stop and think. What are we good at? What did we dream of doing as a kid? What still fascinates us and causes us to dream? The answers to these relatively simple questions dredged up from our subconscious or our memory or where ever we store this stuff. Now let's think deeply about how we can use these gifts and leanings to incorporate them more fully within our day-today experience. Indeed, for some of us, we may earn a living out of this; for others, this may be down the road. But for others, finding a way of occupying ourselves within our recreational or spare time would be sufficient. This is important because if our free moments are not settled in pursuits we feel passionate about, the years of our existence roll on. As our passions dwindle, a deep sense of dissatisfaction begins to form. Without adequately examining the cause and effect of this process, we can find ourselves filling the gaps with all kinds of useless, even destructive stuff. The hole only widens because we are all here for a purpose. I believe that discovering and living our life purpose is imperative if we are fulfilled as people. And I think that personal fulfillment in this context is so fundamentally necessary because without it, our self-worth suffers, and low self-worth coupled with pointlessness produces people with nothing to live for. Suppose you're living your life and you feel there is no objective behind it. In that case, your moral compass will be affected, your relationships will be affected, and your ability to inspire hope in others will be significantly reduced. But once you regain a sense that you count and invest in that reality and live to realize what you were put on the planet for, not only do the possibilities of your life open up, but also your personal sense of fulfillment. The meaning will make for a considerably happier, healthier life. So discover your life purpose and eliminate everything that drains your selfworth. Cultivate habits and behaviors that enhance the sense that you're making a meaningful contribution. And enjoy the journey.

CHAPTER 3

INCREASE YOUR SELF-WORTH NOW

We all know how strong self-worth is. You don't have to be a scientist to realize that the way you perceive yourself, the world will perceive you.

Success goes hand in hand with one's healthy self-worth. I say healthy, as there can be a fine line where self-worth becomes one of the attributes of an ego-driven personality. Where healthy self-worth turns into ever-attention-seeking and demanding 'unhealthy' narcissism or self-centeredness, this is not a way to success and can be a pitfall to someone unaware.

 However, today I am not going to talk about increasing your ego, but rather the sense of the self-worth of your real being (real YOU), which is stable, nurturing, kind and loving. I'll give you some insights into understanding the traps of ego domination. Ego loves to be in the center of attention, feel important and be in charge of others or, in other words, manipulative. Yet it appears robust, but it is not. When you follow celebrities, you can see how often their self - worth turns into their fall as maintaining ever-increasing demands of ego is complicated. To achieve success and then be a slave to it requires a lot of energy.

Success can become unhealthy, and when ego takes over, they turn to drugs, self-pity, and other degrading activities. The unhealthy self-worth (or toxic pride) of ego will not last or make someone happy. The ego is of an animal nature, based on emotions, and is too quick to turn, so the sense of stability is something the ego can't ever give you.

The ego can give you a false sense of increased self-worth and unhealthy low self-worth. Unhealthy low self-worth (or feeling of unworthiness) is also harmful to you and other people around you.

The trustworthy source of success, health, and happiness come from the higher Self, not from the ego. Your higher or spiritual Self is your objective, so never settle for less. Once you see this, it will transform how you look at life, people, and, most importantly you.

The perception of yourself is the key to increasing your selfworth. The more connection you can find with your higher Self, the more self-worth you will establish. Once you know that you are an eternal being and not just an appearance in this temporary temple, which is called the body, you will find your way to a deep appreciation of everything that you are and, at the same deep compassion toward all of your shortcomings too.

You are worthy and have always been beyond understanding of your mind, which you must uncover every day, bit by bit. Everyone, including you, plays a crucial part in the world to succeed. Everything gets noted in the universe, your successes and errors you make on the way. We all learn, and today we are learning more about self-worth

.

3 Simple Tips To Increase Your Self-Worth:

☐ Stop That 'Negative Thinking.'

The feeling of self-doubt can overtake you unexpectedly. Somebody may say something, or some unforeseen events happen. The ego likes to make you believe that your thoughts are YOU or what you think you are. However, this is not true. We pick up ideas in the form of energy and in the way we are being; we have access to thought from the energy field to which we belong.

So when you feel thoughts of negative nature, try to enter your mind, don't let them in. I know this may be hard to do, as it requires a high degree of awareness, but at the start, even when they enter into your mind, let them go past you without any attachment or involvement, and don't claim them as your own. Refer to them as thoughts that have nothing to do with you. View them as just data passing through your mind and don't get any desire to entertain them. The ego loves suffering and loves thinking. Thinking is what it thrives on, predominantly negative reviews. The more drama it can create, the more entertaining it is, and so it gets a lot of pleasure out of being a victim, being unworthy, being 'poor me,' being 'look how bad all is, nobody likes me, nobody wants me' and so on and on.

Catch this tendency early enough, and be honest, did you ask for these thoughts in the first place? You didn't, I'm sure; they just entered your mind. Don't claim them as yours if you didn't ask for them. Be strong and train yourself. The brain is made for thinking, yet you are more than just a brain; you are the master of YOU.

❑ Connect With Your Higher Self

You will develop a close and substantial connection by gaining knowledge about your Higher (spiritual) Self. The higher Self is connected to the Higher Divine Power (or you may call God). This Higher Power makes you worthy no matter what. It is the natural source of your life.

The easiest way to get to it is through simple ways of being with yourself and others. Like for example, the feeling of appreciation is compelling. Some people misunderstand the feeling of unconditional love, as many mix it up with personal honey (attachment, owning, or controlling), and it is not the same.

Unconditional love toward yourself and all life is an ultimate shortcut to connection with the Higher Power.

☐ Use Practical And Straightforward Methods

You can use many practical methods to develop a sense of self-worth. It depends on the situation; many times people become very passive when they feel self-doubt. Simple things like daily exercise change the chemistry of your mind and body, uplift you and make you feel worthy. Never underestimate the simple and practical approaches to a healthy body and mind. A healthy body is a healthy mind, and a practical reason is obedience to your unique authentic (Higher Self). With the support of your strong body, mind, and spiritual will' you become unstoppable and very powerful indeed.

Self-worth becomes second nature. It is healthy and uplifts others too. A fantastic tool for connecting to your spiritual

Self is meditation. It can be challenging to start with, as people often can't master the mind or themselves. It is proper training for your mind, increases your self-worth and intelligence, and changes the brain's chemistry. In the beginning, I felt frustrated. However, I was so desperate to succeed that I didn't give up. Once mastered, now I'm looking forward to it every day. It is a truly fantastic experience.

Self-worth is natural and given to you as a gift. Treasure, nurture, and appreciate it. Be kind and forgiving not only to others but also to yourself. Through love, kindness, gratitude, and forgiveness, self-worth presents itself with grace, elegance, and ease every time. Find and use positive affirmations; use anything that helps you every time selfdoubt sets in.

Lift your mood and surrender to the Higher Power ALL that you seem to lose power over every single time. Go ahead and use the tips; you will be amazed at your great, newly found self-worth, my friend.

CHAPTER 4

SELF-WORTH - YOUR SUCCESS DEPENDS ON IT

"Self-worth, or how you feel about yourself, is our most important possession."

Rainer Martens

Self-Worth: Your Success Depends On It

Even though our society seems restrained in discussions about Self-Worth, it needs to be included as part of everybody's success plans and strategies. It already affects all of us-in a negative, neutral, or positive way-so. Let's have Self-Worth as part of our awareness program.

And what about our children? The percentage of teenagers who attempt suicide in North America is now at an all-time high.

It is part of your personality that determines personal value and importance. Deeply seated within you, it strongly influences your attitudes and the behaviors affecting your success or failure.

When self-worth is low, people have little or no energy to think, feel, and do. They lack the motivation to participate in life.

Here is an example from my own life. Over 16 years ago (before meeting my wife), I was engaged to an individual from Australia. After spending almost a year in my area, she returned home to plan for our wedding. Two months later, she contacted me with one of those Dear John phone calls. After that phone call, my self-worth hit my lowest point. Almost in total depression, I did not eat. In the next 30 days, I lost 15 pounds. Following that phone call, I went from being our company's number-one sales performer to the poorest performer in fewer than 60 days.

High self-worth creates the opposite results. With high sclfworth, people believe their efforts will make a difference wherever they become involved. This high self-worth results in confidence that increase their success.

That is true for all of us-and, especially our kids.

Recent research supports that our self-worth levels are constantly fluctuating and re-established daily. I suspect even Donald Trump had a few low self-worth days after his bankruptcy. Research also supports that experiencing success produces more success and higher self-worth levels. That's why in sales training, they say that the best time for a person to sell something is right after they have just sold something!

How does self-worth affect us?

People with low self-worth experience this challenges. o They claim more emotional problems.
o They expect to be rejected. o They take personal criticism poorly. o They are less comfortable socially. o They are more resistant to change.

Those with high self-worth have this

advantages. o They are less depressed. o They think well of others. o They are more persistent. o They take personal responsibility. o They have more personal flexibility.

Where do you start to improve your self-worth?

As in all situations, the best approach is to take an assessment to establish the required awareness to act and initiate change. When I completed a self-worth assessment many years ago, it helped me understand the concept of situational self-worth levels and how my self-worth varied to the extreme based on the circumstances. In work, I had very high self-worth levels, but with my family of origin, they were pretty low. How could that be?

Self-worth is developed over time within your environment. I was very successful in my work, but in the background of my family life growing up, I had to endure a daily dose of criticism. With low self-worth that carried into my adult life, I became critical of myself until I recognized it for its destructive behavior and altered it! That attitude adjustment helped increase my self-worth in essential areas. That assessment certainly helped change my life.

I want to mention that low self-worth can be biologically generated in some individuals. Yes, based on your diet and blood chemistry, you could have depression or low selfworth based on a biological condition-not, a mental or emotional condition.

This was also true for me many years ago when it was discovered that I was hypoglycemic (low blood sugar), even though several doctors had misdiagnosed me as having manic depression. As you look toward increasing your confidence and self-worth levels, please remember that physiological factors can also affect them.

To get started on this journey, please follow the action steps below.

1. Establish your situational self-worth levels by completing a self-worth assessment.

2. Identify your self-worth in the Self, Family, Peers, Work, and Projected-Self categories.

3. If need be, seek help from others or a professional counselor.

4. Learn more about who you are; recognize your style, values, and needs.

5. Develop respect for yourself.

6. Forgive yourself.

7. Take personal responsibility for your improvement

CHAPTER 5

EGO AND HOW TO BUILD AND IMPROVE YOUE SELF WORTH

According to Freud ego is an essential aspect of humanity. Over the years, ego has become equated to one's sense of self and more often related to one's importance in life. Most often, it was assumed how to build and improve self-worth was to make one's importance. The more important you were, the greater your ego and self-worth.

In fact, for many who want to know how to build and improve self-worth, this is still the model that many use.

The problem with self-importance is that one generally becomes addicted to it like an addict to a drug. Arrogance leads to a strong ego and the need to prove one's importance to oneself and others continually. In extreme, strong egos start wars and manipulate others for their agenda. Strong egos thrive on being more significant than others, more intelligent than others, and superior to others.

They make hideous greedy monarchs that rule with an iron hand and destroy anyone who disagrees with them. But most with high egos don't make it to become a monarch of a country. They become monarchs to their companies, families, social organizations, and so on.

But do those with high egos have a high level of self-worth? The answer is, "No, they have no self-worth." And the reason is this: They are never satisfied with what they have in life and constantly have to demonstrate and prove their importance. And to this end, they often are greedy, take unfair advantage of others, or manipulate others to prove their self-importance.

Those with high egos are often very possessive and can easily be jealous of others. They are likewise incapable of unconditional love.

So it would make sense that a person with a low ego would have a high level of self-worth. No, a low ego is only a prerequisite to a high level of self-worth. The problem is that those with low egos generally feel inferior and bad about themselves. They often don't like themselves and have no self-worth.

So we're in a catch-22 situation. However, it can be said that it's easier for a person with a low ego to build self-worth than for someone with a high ego. The reason is that a person with a high ego is addicted to manipulating and controlling others and may likewise be addicted to greediness.

Just how is self-worth built? To do so, moving to a different game in town is essential. Those who make self-worth by creating ego or self-importance usually strive to excel at something. Their ego and self-worth depend on their ability to maintain that level of superiority. If they lose whatever they have built their ego upon, they drop into a mid-life crisis and have no self-worth while in the situation.

What is the different game? Answer: Self-worth is something that is built day after day. We all have goals and feel good about ourselves when we achieve them. That's the easy part and is no different than what we've been doing all our lives.

Rather than get into self-put-downs for making mistakes, you learn how to feel and experience the disappointments and stop being your disappointment. Instead, choose to like you no matter what my writings are about.

What is the different game? Answer: Self-worth is something that is built day after day. We all have goals and feel good about ourselves when we achieve them. That's the easy part and is no different than what we've been doing all our lives. The problem is that life is more often about the plans (goals) that fall through-the disappointments in life.

The goal is to feel good about yourself when your plans fall through. Feel good about yourself on a "bad hair day." Rather than get into self-put-downs for making mistakes, you learn how to feel and experience the disappointments and stop being your disappointment. Instead, choosing to like you no matter what is how to build and improve selfesteem the right way. Yes, throw away your ego and instead learn how to develop and enhance self-worth--your life will be far more rewarding.

CHAPTER 6

HOW TO BOOST SELF-WORTH AND FEEL BETTER ABOUT YOURSELF

Self-worth is the value you place on yourself. As with anything of value, the worth you put on yourself can rise and fall based on events in your life and situations you are facing. When you ask yourself how much you are worth, the answer you give is your self-worth.

There are many ways to improve your self-worth and how you feel about yourself, even though you may have ups and downs.

The mere fact that you exist gives you value, whether you want to believe that. You were created with your own set of strengths, skills, ideas, and talents.

If you think of self-worth in terms of financial worth, it becomes easier to understand how you can increase your own cost. If you wanted more money, you would take specific actions to get a raise at work or make certain decisions within your business to increase its value. The same holds for your self-worth. If you want to improve it, you have to invest in yourself.

To begin increasing your self-worth, here are some actions you can take right now:

1.) Start a hobby. The more things that you can do - and do well - the better you will feel about yourself. The skills you have are a significant determining factor of your self-worth. Consider adding to your list of hobbies or recreational activities to boost your self-worth.

• When you enjoy the things you do in life, you want yourself more!

2.) Learn something new. Taking a class is a great way to add value to yourself. Adding knowledge to your mind is like depositing money in the bank.

• Check with your local community college for classes that interest you.

• Sign up for an online class or seminar.

• Take a community education class through your local school district. They offer many types across a wide range of subjects and are affordable.

3.) Open a book. Reading is a fantastic way to stimulate your mind. When your imagination is at work, it helps to spark new ideas. Learning more about the world around you will build self-worth.

• Research a topic you are interested in learning more about or have always wanted to try.

4.) Learn a new language. There are several ways to go about mastering a new language, from the internet to audio courses, to college classes. Not only will the challenge build your self-worth, but the ability to communicate with others on a different level is advantageous.

5.) Expand your comfort zone. Doing something out of the ordinary broadens your horizons and makes you a more interesting individual. You will also be surprised at what you can do when you try something you never thought you would.

Self-confidence and self-worth are closely tied together. When you feel better about yourself and what you can achieve, you place a higher value on yourself, and your selfworth rises. And the opposite is also true; when your selfworth is down, your self-confidence diminishes.

To boost your self-worth, commit to choosing one of the activities above to see what a difference it makes for yourself.

CHAPTER 7

INCREASING YOUR SELF-WORTH - IT IS TIME TO VALUE YOU

In this world of self-improvement and self-development, I believe it is essential not to overlook self-worth.

We talk of education, image, money, etc. Most of these things will not hold as much meaning or fulfillment if the issue of low self-worth is not addressed. So, what is selfworth, and why is it essential to increase it?

Your self-worth is your interest in your value or your merit. We can establish your level of self-worth by asking a few simple questions. How valuable do you think you are? For a long time, I looked to others to determine my worth. I looked for men to show me that I was worth being with. I looked to pastors and ministers to validate my gifting and calling. I looked to my children to determine if I had any worth as a parent. I looked everywhere but the one place that mattered. I was trying to establish my price through others, not even realizing that I was showing the world that I saw no value in myself and needed someone to tell me that I was worth something.

Today, I live a life where I am more confident, assured, and validated. Is it because someone finally made me see my worth in myself? No, It is because I finally decided to stop searching on the outside for my price and start getting to know myself and exploring my inner being.

To know if you have a healthy or high self-worth, answer the following questions.

Are you rarely confident and assured in yourself?

Do you envy others because they have what you will never have?

Do you believe that every "good" thing that happens to you is "too good to be true?"

When life seems harsh, do you go into a shell and hide away or do you stand and know that it will pass?

Do you abuse or allow yourself to be used because you feel you deserve it?

Do you feel that you have to prove yourself to others?

Do you look outside of yourself for validation?

Do you measure your worth by what you possess?

If your answers to these questions were mostly "yes," you need a boost in your self-worth, self-esteem, self-love, and overall self-perception. You must know that your actual value and worth can only begin to increase when you take the step of looking inside.

Here are a few ways that you can begin to increase your self-worth:

Set goals based on what is important to you, not everyone else. You must know what makes your heart sing. If you know the answer to that, you should not let anyone else dictate the importance of it.

- Compliment yourself every day. This is not about conceit. This is about you noticing that there is something extraordinary about you just as well as another.

- Speak positive affirmations to yourself daily. e.i. - I have all I need to live a whole life right here within me.

- Read motivational books regularly. Even if you think most of them are cheesy, they may have the message you need to make it through another day.

- Celebrate every achievement. It is okay to smile when you have accomplished a goal. Again I am not speaking of arrogance; I am speaking of you acknowledging yourself and your value.

- Do something that makes you smile every day. Be it reading, dancing, shopping(moderately if you are on a budget), having a slice of cake, having that peach soda, etc. Simple things add up.

- Be sure about what you want, and do not let anyone talk you out.

- Spend time developing your craft or skills. We all have natural abilities. Know yours and spend time developing them.

- Let go of envy. You do not have to envy another when you know that you are worthy of sound just as much as they are.

- Love others for who they are but establish your individuality. You are unique enough, just as you are.

CHAPTER 8

HOW TO RAISE YOUR SELF-WORTH

Do you find yourself worthy?

Self-worth is your ability to appreciate, accept, and value yourself independent of success, failure, or the opinions of others. It means having an overall favorable view of yourself, believing in your right to feel good, and therefore choosing your thoughts, actions, and expressions based on the belief that you matter.

If you plan to achieve your goals, whether they are goals of weight loss, ending emotional eating, or overcoming stress, sadness, or depression, you will also need to build a good sense of self-worth. While self-worth is not about your achievements, it is about spending energy and effort in pursuits that are meaningful to you and your happier life. When you feel worthy, you feel motivated to make behavior choices that support your overall goals of success and joy.

What is the definition of self-worth? Low self-worth is best described as having a humble opinion of yourself and feeling unworthy. It can result in some common thoughts, actions, and behaviors, including:

" Low motivation

" Feeling stupid, fat, ugly, useless, or unwanted

" A sense of not being good enough or on equal ground with others

" Not feeling strong enough to handle things on your own

" Feeling judged by others

" Needing to be more articulate, prettier, intelligent, prosperous, etc.

" Finding it hard to forgive yourself for making mistakes

Dissatisfaction with life

" Depression

" Low energy levels

" Feeling helpless to change things

" Feeling either superior or inferior to others, never equal

" Withdrawn from social contact

" A sense of defeat and hopelessness

One of the problems of believing yourself to be low selfworthy is that you will act according to your belief. If you think you are unworthy of love, you will work as though you are unworthy of love. If you believe you are an outcast, you will act as if you are an outcast. Your beliefs define your reality. In truth, you are so much more than what you believe about yourself. You are the breath of creation in human form, the combination of spirit and physicality. If you currently have low self-worth, there is hope! You can decide to change it.

Five Ways To Increase Your Self-Worth

Raising self-worth is a very personal and often complex process. There is no one magic formula to make you believe you are a worthy individual. It takes time, effort, and awareness to allow a sense of worth to deepen. Since strengthening your sense of value takes motivation and action, you have to want and choose this as your goal before you can improve it. Dare to love yourself. It is your journey, and without your support, you will not get anywhere.

However, if you are ready, below are a few suggestions that can and will actively build your self-worth.

☐ Realize You Have Control Over Your Future

Encourage yourself to focus on the dreams and desires that are important to you. Begin by permitting yourself to imagine and pretend that you are living your most perfect life. What ideas awaken passion, creativity, intuition, and gut feelings? What makes you laugh, feel good, and come to life? What do you stand for? Once you know what goal or direction is essential, and decide to spend time, energy, and action involved in those pursuits, your sense of worth increases when you become involved with the things necessary to you.

☐ Think Better Thoughts

Begin to notice your automatic thoughts. Are your inner voices supportive and loving, or critical and abusive? Consciously watch your thoughts as a detached observer. There is no need to fight your thoughts, pretend to ignore them, or even judge them. Instead, bring your thoughts out into the open. Acknowledge their existence, write them down, and speak them aloud. Sit back and say, "Isn't that interesting that I am thinking these thoughts." Feeling insecure or anxious is okay, and you still love yourself. Adding the supportive and loving thoughts you want to hear is also OK. Your thoughts are your responsibility, and while you cannot erase opposing thoughts, you can learn to challenge them.

☐ Express Your Self

Self-worth is your ability to feel free to be yourself. So it makes sense that if your self-worth is low, you will likely invest your time role-playing and pretending to be somebody other than you. You will find yourself behaving in ways others expect you to act so that they will like you. Yet, inwardly you will feel self-critical and judgmental and believe yourself to be different in some non-okay way. It is your right to be who you are, express your innermost truths, and not feel like you must live up to someone else's expectations. You have the right to say "No" when you mean no, or "I don't care" when that is what you feel inside. However, self-worth also includes your decision to communicate directly, state your preferences and opinions, and speak in a concise assertive voice.

☐ To Err Is Human

Self-worth is your ability to acknowledge your strengths and weaknesses while at the same time accepting yourself as worthy and worthwhile. If you want to raise your self-worth, let yourself gain a realistic perspective about mistakes, obstacles, setbacks, and failure. Failure is the only way to become successful. Although no one wants to experience failure, you can remind yourself that failure is a natural aspect of every successful journey. Think of misfortunes as temporary and specific instead of permanent and general. In other words, your current effort may have been unsuccessful, but that doesn't mean your overall goal or dream is unattainable. Learn from your setback, revise your action plan, and begin again.

5. Be Responsible for Your Success

Raising your self-worth includes being responsible for your happiness and success. To achieve this, learn to be your best friend and supporter. Constantly tell yourself what a good job you are doing. Actively seek out evidence of your success. Praise your efforts. Learn to be excited by your choices. Recognize your many triumphs - however small they may seem. Self-worth is the overflowing of love and acceptance from within you directed to you. Decide you will allow yourself to feel successful with each step you take, no matter what the outcome is. It is enough that you have taken the stage. You are enough.

Self-worth is your right to live and be happy. Follow these steps, and you will find that you have set into motion forces that allow you to deepen your sense of self-worth. Good luck and good self-worth!

CHAPTER 9

BEGIN BUILDING A SENSE OF SELFWORTH AND OVERCOME BEING IN THE DUMPS

A Course in Miracles asks us to "Concern ourselves with the holiness that we truly are." And that being said, and sad to say that, much of the world still seems to suffer from a low sense of self-worth.

Yet even though some individuals appear to have been born with a great deal of self-esteem, this is not the case, although healthy self-esteem originates from youth.

Kids affected by loving and caring parents and other grownups who put in the time to impart a sense of self-worth will become confident grownups.

Kids who do not grow up in a positive environment will likely suffer the pain of low self-esteem in adulthood. They will feel severe about themselves and lack the selfconfidence to realize their goals and dreams.

In the Dumps We cannot get out of the dumps or slumps we're in without having peace of mind, and to do so, we must be listening to the self-worth in our hearts.

A Course in Miracles states, "This a year of joy, in which your listening will increase, and peace will grow with its increase."

The worst part of all is that low self-confidence is entirely incorrect.

Everyone is unique, with special skills and gifts nobody can provide.

Convincing an individual with low self-confidence that they are unique is not simple, but it is vital in reconstructing their sense of self-worth and value to the world.

Positive Self-Esteem

It's practically certain that they will, if we expect people to think of us in an unfavorable way.

Improving self-confidence starts with changing the way you believe about yourself.

You will naturally develop self-confidence and sense of selfworth by minimizing negative ideas and increasing favorable ones.

It can require time and hard work to let go of harmful youth affects and rebuild self-esteem. With aid and persistence, anybody can improve their self-confidence and worth. Low Self-Esteem Help The effort will be rewarded with a higher sense of worth and the self-confidence to fulfill goals and pursue more significant and much better things.

Remember, it's so essential for us to see that youngsters who are influenced by truly loving parents and other adults, like coaches and teachers, and so many other influential people, who take the time to talk about the better things in life, give kids a greater chance to grow into positive adults.

Convincing an individual who may appear to be down in the dumps that they are unique is not easy, but it is essential in shining the light on their sense of self-worth.

By reducing wrong-minded negative ego-based ideas, we begin increasing right-minded, more intrinsically favorable ones, and you will naturally start building self-confidence and a great deal of your sense of self-worth and value to the world.

CHAPTER 10

SELF-WORTH: IS SELF-WORTH SOMETHING WE DEVELOP?

On one side, it could be said that there is confidence, and on the other, it could be said that there is self-worth. The first could be seen as something one can experience at one level, and the other could be seen as something one can experience at another level.

Therefore, even though one is confident, it doesn't mean one value themselves, and although one can love themselves, it doesn't mean one will always come across as though they are full of confidence. This doesn't mean one can't have both, but it does mean that one thing doesn't always lead to the other.

An Analogy

For example, a cake can look magnificent, but that doesn't mean it tastes as good as it seems. It could be said that it is easier to make a cake look good than to create a cake taste good.

This is similar to how it is often easier for someone to develop confidence than for them to develop self-worth.

However, while confidence can come and go, self-worth is not as transitory.

Feedback

Confidence is often something that one experiences through receiving feedback from others. For instance, one can have their hair done, and then people can tell them how good they look, and one can then feel confident.

Another way this can happen is when other people tell them they have done an excellent job. Through receiving their feedback, one can end up feeling confident.

Fleeting

Once they have received this feedback from others, they can feel on top of the world, and then as time passes, the feelings, thoughts, and sensations they are experiencing can start to disappear. This can then cause one to come crashing down, and they may feel the need to do something else to gain more positive feedback from others.

However, if one values themselves, it will be possible for them to feel good without needing constant feedback from others. When they experience a change in their emotional state, they are unlikely to have the same need to find another way to share positive feedback

Constant Feedback

If one is in an environment where they receive constant feedback, they may come across as though they are not only confident, but they value themselves. Yet, if they were to spend time alone or be around people who don't give them the same responses, they might soon come crashing down. For instance, when one needs constant feedback on how they look, it is likely to show that they haven't developed their self-worth. And as they don't value themselves, they need other people to give them what they can't give themselves; however, it won't be possible for them to internalize what they hear.

Grounded Confidence

As a result of how they feel about themselves, they are unlikely to act as though they are more critical than others. This is because they will be operating as a whole human being instead of being stuck in their head.

When one doesn't value themselves, and their confidence is based on how other people respond to them, it can mean that they are out of touch with their body. It can then be normal for them to have an exaggerated sense of importance.

The Mind

This will be because they are out of touch with their shame, and it will then be a challenge for them to have a grounded sense of themselves. Without the body's shame to keep the mind in check, it will be expected for one to get caught up in the illusions that the mind creates.

This shows how important it is for one to not only focus on their mind when it comes to developing self-worth, but also on their body. It could be said that the most critical area to focus on is the body.

A Common Outlook

It is often said that our self-worth is defined by what we believe, and this can then cause us to focus on our mind. This also creates the impression that one can develop self-worth by having the correct beliefs.

They can then end up using affirmations, positive thinking, and success as a way to change their beliefs. However, there is a strong chance that this will cause one to cover up how they truly feel, and as was motioned above, this can cause them to create a false-self.

Another Perspective

Another way of looking at this would be to say that it is not so much that one needs to develop self-worth, as it is they one need to realize their self-worth. This is because it is not something they can develop; it is an inherent part of who they are.

One's self-with is something that will be found in their body and not their mind; however, for one to realize this, one will need to work through the pain that is in their body. Once they get in touch with this pain, they will likely see that they are carrying toxic shame.

Toxic Shame

Behind toxic shame is going to be their inherent worth, but all the time they are carrying this, it will not be possible for them to realize their intrinsic value. This cannot be changed by thinking or behaving differently, and it won't change through achieving success, either.

Awareness

One way to let go of their toxic shame will be to face how they feel and tolerate the charge until it begins to discharge. Being around people who affirm their inherent worth will also be an essential part of this process.

Toxic shame can only survive when it is being covered up, and this is why it is so essential for one to shine a light on this part of themselves. The assistance of a therapist and a support group is likely to be needed here.

CHAPTER 11

SELF-WORTH - HOW CAN I FEEL SPECIAL?

Do you feel you do not matter much and have little to offer? What's the point you ask yourself of making an effort? "Whatever, I say won't make much of a difference, and I won't be noticed." These are signs of low self-worth. Such a way of seeing oneself can lead to a depressive mind.

There are several ways in which people value themselves and assess their selfworth.

Comparison With Others And Self-Worth

The common thing is to look for some way you are better than others. Perhaps you have a more competent car, a more extensive garden, or more fashionable clothes. Or maybe you are socially popular or well-known for what you do at work. The Western world values winners - being more physically attractive, educationally advanced, or financially successful.

But not everyone can beat the competition. There is always someone more affluent, better thought of, or more influential than you or me. We can't all be at the top of the pile. And measuring oneself against others means that your sense of self-worth will rise and fall in step with your latest success or failure.

Research at the University of Michigan found that the students who reported more stress, anger, academic problems, and relationship conflicts based their self-worth on comparison with others on external things such as academic performance, physical appearance, and being socially approved. Self-appreciation and a sense of one's unique strengths and qualities mattered for a sense of selfworth. Some of these may not be valued by others. So how can one appreciate oneself when few do?

Doing Meaningful Things And Self-Worth

What is meaningful in life varies according to individual interest and experience, but doing something that you happen to value can help with self-worth. Studies are finding that helping others and volunteering positively affect how people feel about themselves.

Doing things for only external reasons can be demoralizing when the rewards don't come; a bonus from the company, or tip from a customer that didn't materialize, or the unforthcoming offer of employment from someone you are trying to impress. However, the worker who values getting a job done well and on time feels good about him- or herself even when the client or boss fails to show any thanks or praise. Everyone needs a few gratitude from time to time. Being appreciated is what can keep us going. But when you depend upon it, you perhaps need to think again about what you set store by in what you do; what is essential about your input.

Adding Value To A Situation And Self-Worth

What seems to matter to self-worth is the attitude one brings to everyday activities and relationships - not just at work but in the home and community. If you attach importance to generosity, how generous is your attitude to those who need a little of your time? If you value patience in life, how patient are you with children? If you love home life, how supportive are you of your family? I would suggest that the more your ways of living are in harmony with the values you cherish, the more self-worth you will feel.

Unique Contribution And Self-Worth

Every person you meet can walk away from you, feeling just a little happier. This can be because of the way you deal with them, the effort you put in, and the interest you have shown. Feeling their appreciation if you get it is part of the delight.

To my way of thinking, it doesn't matter in what circumstance you find yourself - at home, work, or play - there will always be an opportunity to add value to the situation by what you choose to say and do. What this is will vary according to who you are - not only your values but your strengths, experience, and disposition, for everyone brings something slightly different and unique to the table. No two people have the same way of being useful where there is a need. It might be a thoughtful suggestion, a warmth of concern, a sense of humor, an appropriate piece of relevant knowledge, a relevant personal experience, a practical action, a sensitive empathy, or a wise insight. The list could go on.

Spiritual teachings and self-worth

Feeling good about what you do is very different from feeling you are good. A spiritual perspective acknowledges some higher power beyond that of human beings. According to this view, all people who behave well, whatever their race, education, and background, are united because there is an infinite creative force behind all that is humane in the world. I believe that all the worthwhile things we do are a result of being a willing channel for this higher power. I am not good, but can feel good because the more I put into a situation, the more I will get out of it as I experience the inflow of energy, fulfillment, and enlightenment.

CHAPTER 12

3 TIPS TO HELP YOU INCREASE YOUR SENSE OF SELF WORTH

Many gurus might have told you that you need to increase your sense of self-worth before you can amount to anything in life, which would be true.

And other things related to self-worth would be selfconfidence, self-esteem, and other similar terms related to your mental health.

The truth is, psychiatrists have found out that your sense of self-worth has a direct impact on your success in life, which is why individuals with unhealthy self-worth levels tend to get nowhere in life.

Don't let that happen to you. If you're struggling, I have some tips below to help with your self-worth.

Tip 1 - Learning To Say No!

If you say "yes" all the time to people, watch out.

People who say "yes" all the time tend to feel lousy about themselves, so to gain the approval of others, they resort to saying "yes" all the time to whatever requests they get.

But if you have a strong and healthy sense of self-worth, you won't need to prove to others how good you are. You'll feel secure about yourself.

Saying "yes" to everyone will only burn you out, and it will do you no good in the end. Instead, build your sense of selfworth, and you won't always feel the need to oblige to requests thrown at you.

Tip 2 - Take Up A New Hobby Or Learn A New Skill

Sometimes, picking up new additional skills help when you're building up your sense of self-worth, because you always feel good when you know you have something extra to offer to the world.

But you need to be careful not to pick up those skills just to please others. It's OK if it's something you are interested in, but don't do it to please others.

To ensure you don't fall into that trap, start with your hobbies because that's starting from your passion, not the pressure from others. Then work your way up from there.

And also, don't procrastinate. Procrastination is a sign of a low sense of self-worth because you fear failure coming your way. So you rather stay put than risk failure.

Step out and give it a go. If you're starting from a passion, you'll have fun along the way, even if you meet with failure.

Tip 3 - Always Give Your Best

It's always difficult to understand why some people never give their best, no matter their task. And because they produce something sloppy, they are demanded to re-perform the job.

And what happens when they still don't meet the mark after several times? They end up with the mentality that they aren't good enough for the task and will never amount to anything in life.

Can you see how that's a vicious cycle? It can happen to you, too, if you're not careful.

Of course, it's understandable if you're naturally not gifted for that task, but we're referring to the attitude of not giving your best even before starting on your given task, creating that vicious cycle.

Believe me, if you do your best for a task, even if it's something you're unfamiliar with, you'll still end up with something acceptable, not something that comes across as sloppy.

Giving your best also gets you out of the vicious cycle of wasting more time redoing stuff, and that not only saves you tons of energy and wonders for your sense of self-worth because you know you're not a loser in life.

Can you now see how your sense of self-worth can be improved using the tips above? They might be simple tips, but apply them, and you'll be amazed at how they will help you.

CHAPTER 13

HOW TO DEAL WITH LOW SELF-ESTEEM - WAYS TO REGAIN YOUR SELF-WORTH

Since we recently discussed the symptoms of low selfesteem in another article, it made sense also to discuss how to deal with it. As a quick review for those that haven't read the report, the symptoms of low self-esteem are: **1)** A firm belief that you are somehow "worth less" than those around you.

2) Trying to live someone else's life instead of your own. **3)** Accepting when other people treat you as less than human.

4) Taking on other people's "stuff" to have them like you more.

5) Convincing yourself that it isn't that bad or that it's all somehow required of you.

Before we begin, we though it would be a good idea to ensure that we're all on the same page with what Self-Esteem means. That way, we could also help eliminate some of the confusion about what it is. In most simple terms...

SelfEsteem is the internal belief that we have worth and value in our own life.

This takes us to the first thing you can do to build self-esteem in your own life - stop looking to others to give you selfesteem. As we defined in the definition, self-esteem is internal. As soon as you try to get it from someone else, it works to undermine any self-esteem you may have developed. This is because you must sell yourself out to justify the power you're trying to give to the other person or people. This doesn't mean you can't build self-esteem by working "with" others. Helping others is often a great tool to add depth and meaning to our lives.

The next thing you can do is to have dreams and goals, and to set expectations for yourself. If you live your life in neutral, without any direction, then your life will be "purpose-less" and "meaning-less." Having dreams and goals, it gives you something to work towards, as well as gives you something you can use to chart your progress. The key is to set all sorts of goals, big and small, and to expect yourself to meet them - or at least come as close as possible. If you just set goals but don't also put an expectation on yourself to meet them; then it becomes the same as not setting goals in the first place.

On top of that, you need to be dedicated to yourself and pay attention to your actions. If you ignore the things you do, how can you know what you're doing? In the equal measure, you could be doing good things for yourself or selling yourself out. If you sell yourself out, self-esteem can't possibly grow, not to mention it will also cause your selfesteem to diminish - if you have any, that is. That is also the secret to being dedicated to yourself; to focus on your best interests and be committed to yourself.

From this point, you also need to do what needs to be done right away - don't procrastinate. As soon as something needs to be done, or you want to do do it (use common sense on what's acceptable to do and what isn't). If you don't do it, then you will see again self yourself out. This can be as simple as wanting to get a glass of water or as complex as ensuring you get to work on time. If we waste time and do not do the things we want to or need to do, then we have to tell ourselves "I'm not worth the effort!" to undermine them. How can you ever have or build self-esteem if you're not worth your effort?

This goes hand-in-hand with the next thing you need to do - show yourself you have worth and value every day. This can be as simple as doing and following the other things we've discussed. It can also include having "Me Time,"; which means doing things for yourself that add depth and meaning to your life. That can consist of reading books, pursuing a hobby, being creative, exploring art, or just about anything else. "Me Time" doesn't need to be done daily - it depends on what it is and how long it takes. However, you still need to prove to yourself you have worth every day through your actions. Telling yourself, you have worth doesn't by itself do anything.

That then takes us to the final thing you can do to build selfesteem and worth in your life - Remember You Are Worth Your Own Time And Effort! This is the crucial thing that tie everything together and allows you to succeed at building self-worth. If you are not worth your own time and effort, everything else will be undone, and self-esteem will disappear from your life.

CHAPTER 14

DISCOVER YOUR SELF-WORTH

Have you discovered your self-worth? The answer to this question for most of us will likely be no. If you go through life measuring the self-worth of others by their worldly attachments, you likely measure your self-worth by the same criteria.

Think about this for a moment. When you see a homeless person, do you judge them by the state they are presently in? Does it ever cross your mind that deep inside that person is something so unique that it can change the life of thousands? You see, in life, you are always trying to get something, be it a better job, money, a bigger house, or other material pleasures. You begin to measure your self-worth by the value of your stuff.

I want you to understand that there is nothing wrong with having nice things. You have to ensure you do not allow your possessions to define who you are. If your self-worth is defined by your accomplishments and controls, you will live an unsatisfying life. Your self-esteem will rise and fall with each action and failure, with each control obtained and each control lost.

You have to learn to define your own self-worth by saying things like, "I am a person of great value. I am not defined by my accomplishment, my failures, my possessions, or lack there of. I am created with a divine purpose to impact the life of others."

You must understand that material achievements can never define your true self-worth. They may give you a temporary boost of self-esteem, but when the newness wears off, you will find yourself right back where you started.

Nothing outside of you can bring true self-worth because self-worth always comes from within. You must realize that you are the most important person on this planet to do what you were created to do.

When you connect your self-worth to your possessions, you are doing yourself a disservice. You are better than anything you could ever possess. Regardless of the condition you find yourself in today, you are still more valuable than you can imagine. Many are waiting on you to discover your selfworth, and they are desperate for the gifts you have to offer. I encourage you to begin each day with a healthy breakfast of self-encouragement. Proclaim the greatness within you and allow your creative passion to shine through to enable others to benefit from it. Discovering your own self-worth will enable you to enjoy all that life has to offer.

CHAPTER 15

SELF WORTH - 5 LAWS TO LIVE BY

The suffering of feelings of low self-worth is needless. So many people struggle with low self-esteem. They walk around, living as if they do not belong on the planet. The idea of "being sorry for being alive" is their mode of operation. They often feel inadequate or not good enough.

If you struggle with feelings of low self-worth, congratulate yourself for searching for some answers. Your suffering does not have to last forever.

According to Claudia A. Howard (1992), there are five basic laws of human worth:

- ❖ All have infinite, internal, eternal, and unconditional worth as persons. Your worth is not something that will end. It lives inside of you as the "core self." You, as a core self or spiritual self, will go on forever. Your worth as a human being does not change based on any conditions inside or outside of you.

- ❖ All have equal worth as people. Worth is not comparative or competitive. You are not worth more or less than another person, regardless of skills or abilities. Comparisons cannot take place between two people who have the same worth. Because all humans have the same price, there can be no competition and no winners or losers.

- ❖ Externals neither add to nor diminish worth. Externals are things outside of our core self. These include possessions, performance, circumstances, events, behavior, or looks. Of course, we might wish to work on and improve these things, but only to increase our "market" or "social" worth.

- ❖ This distinction between your human worth and the externals is sometimes challenging to grasp but crucial to your sense of self-worth. When you are born, you have all of the attributes necessary for life. Some of these are developed, and some are not. Your externals, such as how much money you have, your status among others, and the kind of work you do, can either hide or display your core self. For example, making a mistake might make it difficult for you to experience yourself as a worthy and whole person.

- ❖ Worth is stable and never in jeopardy (even if someone rejects you.) Your worth as a human being does not change, ever. Even if every person on this planet said you were worthless, it could not be accurate.

- ❖ Worth doesn't have to be earned or proved. It already exists within you. It is not something to be bought or gained. You cannot have too much of it. Other people do not have to see it for you to have it or believe in it.

The most important thing you can do to boost your selfworth is to learn how to separate your core self-worth from the externals in your life. Begin to recognize the times when you compare yourself to others. Remind yourself then that you are not worth more or less than they are. Welcome the circumstances in your life as opportunities to value yourself and esteem yourself as a worthy person, regardless of your externals.

For example, a young man named Mark worked at an insurance company. He prided himself on the hard work that he did for the company. A new position had opened up, and he gladly interviewed, knowing in his heart that he was the best man for the job. A few days later, Mark noticed another employee had been selected to take this position. Mark went home discouraged that day. He thought to himself how worthless he was. Luckily, his best friend noticed the shift in mood. He reminded Mark that he just needed to work on his skills and that he was still a wonderful, worthy human being. You can be in any circumstance, have many skills or very few, be "good looking" or "frumpy," rich or poor. Your best friend could have just rejected you. The good news is that you will always be worth something, no matter what.

Developing Self-Worth - Tips For Being True To Yourself

Tip 1 - Become Someone Else

If you want to change your life in a natural way, you must be prepared to change as a person. Whatever has sapped your confidence, self-respect, and self-worth must be changed. Now, you can make cosmetic changes, such as a new relationship or job, but if you don't make big inner changes to the person you are, you will still fall into the old patterns.

I think, act, and am completely different to the one I described above.

Suggestion: Don't think of your character as set in stone; think of yourself as a work in progress and very much in charge of that process. You can change your character any time you wish, and if you do, your thoughts, actions, and reactions will vary.

Tip 2 - Take Control Of Your Thoughts

Your mind is not a runaway train in your head, nor a nebulous object floating outside your reach. Your mind is in your head and under your control. You can choose what you think about every minute of every hour of every day. And the type of thoughts you think will change how you feel inside. The more you practice positive reviews, the better you will feel. Happy people feel more substantial, and they have more life energy, as such, they are better at tackling challenges than people who are emotionally and mentally exhausted by sad and complex thoughts.

Exercise: Every time you think of something that makes you feel miserable, angry, or sad, make a conscious decision to stop and think about one of the happiest times of your life. Create that memory in as much detail as you can; feel how happy you felt at that time. Do this every time you think negative.

Tip 3 - Stop Listening To Others

The world and its brother will have opinions about you, but if you want to rebuild yourself into a person who has selfworth via self-confidence and self-respect, then you need to pull back into yourself and start making your own decisions.

Yes, maybe you were a specific person yesterday, but as of now, you have just changed as you are reading this. It's vitally important, if you are to succeed, that you own this fully as your process. For the first time in your life,, you will consciously define yourself.

Remember: Those confident people you envy have made up their minds about who they are, and while they have the confidence to listen to others, they only take on what they hear if it feels right for them to do so. As of now, you are one of those people.

Tip 4 - The A, B, And C List

I was taught this years ago, and the concept has served me well. You need to assess the people in your life at every step.

This is not to say judge them, but make self-protective decisions about the people you know. We, humans, tend to declare random people to be friends and to believe that our close family will love and like us no matter what; sadly, this is often not the case. However, with no lack of love towards fallible human beings, you must make vital decisions about who you listen to.

A   **List:** People who you trust entirely to have your best interests at heart. They know you very well and are honest but supportive. You will always listen and more than likely act on their advice.

B   **List:** People you like, you may come to trust them entirely, but you're not sure how well they know you or how loyal they are, so you will listen but make a judgment call.

C List: They are not your tribe, they don't have your best interests at heart, and you will not listen to them. If you use this idea, you will find it much easier to be yourself. And that is the key to self-worth.

Tip 5 - Breathe And Forgive

There are 7 billion people on this planet, not one of whom is perfect. Sad as it is if you research, you will discover questions about even the greatest spiritual leaders, such as

Gandhi, Martin Luther King, and Mother Theresa. They were human, and like us, not everyone agreed with them. So, you must relax, stop beating yourself up for the mistakes and missteps of the past, and allow yourself to be an ordinary human being.

Thought: One of the most giant blocks to creating self-worth is to keep going over every mistake you've ever made. There comes a time to say, "What's done is done," and move forward. Now is that time.

Developing Self Worth

The tips I've given you above are the foundations for building a new you who trusts and likes yourself. We all have the following:

• The flexibility to define who we are

• The ability to control and direct our thoughts

• The capability to block the negative emotions of others

• The observation skills to be able to decide who we trust

• The need to forgive the past and move forward Next, we need to get real.

People have all kinds of fancy theories as to what selfconfidence and self-worth are, and I would suggest to you that these two things are inextricably linked and together create self-respect and inner strength, but we need to deal with your reality.

The reality is that if you feel bad in any relationship, if you're surrounded by people who don't fully support you if you hate your job, your face, your figure, your home, your car, and your romantic life is a disaster; you will not find it easy to gain self-worth.

However, if you're prepared to change those things one step at a time, and get honest about how you feel about your life, and act on your inner truth no matter what anyone else thinks, you have an excellent chance of changing your life completely, and for the better.

CHAPTER 16

HOW TO BUILD SELF WORTH - WHAT YOU NEED TO KNOW TO BUILD SELF WORTH

You might be wondering what self-worth is; the simplest explanation is self-worth is the value you place on yourself. It's directly linked to having high/ low levels of self-esteem and confidence, so it is essential to continue building your self-worth.

Your self-worth will fluctuate based on different experiences and situations, but there are ways of incrementally building your self-worth through slight lifestyle changes. The key is to focus on doing the things that fill you with positivity and energy and bring about that "feel-good factor."

The following are a few tips for building self-worth daily:

Engage In Activities You Enjoy

It sounds so simple, and it is, yet many don't make enough time to focus on the activities they enjoy. Engage in things that make you feel good about yourself afterward and commit to making time for them daily where feasible.

Learn New Skills

Developing new skill sets is a great way to build self-worth; the more you achieve, the more confidence you'll gain in yourself and your abilities. There are plenty of options for developing new skills and gaining qualifications, such as: * Online coaching and training, such as Open University courses

* Take evening classes at your local college or other means of tuition

Stimulate the mind

The brain is a fantastic tool and can be trained! Reading, for instance, is a great way to stimulate the mind and keep it sharp. Perhaps you could consider writing? If you enjoy writing, you could start blogging and submitting articles just as I am here. How about learning a new language? You could take an online course to learn a new language.

Focus On Your Strengths

Identify the things you're naturally good at and then work on strengthening these areas. Placing too much emphasis on your mistakes and the things you are not so good at will only lower your self-worth; keep working on identifying and developing your strengths. Do something out of the ordinary Step outside your comfort zone once in a while and set yourself new challenges and goals. Engage in things you know you can achieve if you put your mind to it but don't set yourself up for failure. There's no need to go skydiving (unless you want to!), but just set goals that require commitment and are achievable.

To sum up, it's important to remember that self-confidence, self-esteem, and self-worth are all related. Essentially by improving in one area, you're improving in another also; work on improving your self-esteem and your selfconfidence also. Keep striving towards becoming a better, happier, more fulfilled person, and you'll naturally build your self-worth.

CHAPTER 17

IS YOUR NET-WORTH MORE IMPORTANT TO YOU THAN YOUR SELF-WORTH?

I was reflecting recently on the mindsets of several friends and acquaintances who seem willing to sacrifice their selfworth for the uncertainty of their net worth. Why would I say delay in the previous sentence?

I don't care how much money you have in the bank, CDs, your retirement fund, or any other equity in other sources - nothing in the future is ever totally secure, which I'm sure some of you have already discovered.

A high net worth is a worthy goal to work towards, but I would question whether sacrificing your self-worth to achieve it is.

I'm sure you have read at least one book or article that discusses the value of healthy self-worth, so I won't go into great detail here, but the essence of self-worth is you value yourself;

- more than your need for other's value of you
- more than your possessions
- more than the fame or recognition you earn as a result of your achievements
- more than the approval of others
- Self-worth is recognizing and accepting that no matter what you do, accomplish, achieve, or don't, you are valuable for who you are and not what you

do. -Self-worth is accepting that if you fail, you are not less worthy because of your failures but better for attempting something.

- Self-worth believes in yourself and your potential regardless of your education, station in life, contacts, and history.

- Self-worth knows that your opinion of yourself is always more important to you than the opinion of others. -Self-worth is not arrogance or a huge ego but recognizing and accepting your shortcomings or weaknesses as part of being human.

- Self-worth is earned by living an integrity-based life and not achieved due to recognition from others.

- Self-worth is lasting and growing when you focus on the inside-out rather than the outside-in.

- Self-worth isn't diminished because you make mistakes or poor decisions.

- Self-worth is not the result of success but the forerunner to it.

- Self-worth gives you inner peace, contentment, and calm that you are on the right path and all is well no matter what circumstances you are experiencing. -

Self-worth is the ability to look in the mirror and smile at who you are and who you are becoming.

- Self-worth doesn't make excuses or apologize for life circumstances, goals, values, or outcomes.

- Self-worth is always the motive or agenda for goals that reinforce your mission and life purpose.

- And self-worth is humility, knowing that you are following Divine guidance for the rest of your life. I'm sure you could disagree with some or all of the above premises, but I can tell you I have known many people who remained stuck in some area of their life for fear of others' opinions, judgments, or criticism. I have known several people who care more about the views of others of them than their self-opinions. And I have learned many people who refused to believe in themselves and their dreams and accepted the goals of others for them.

CHAPTER 18

WHEN MEN DON'T KNOW THE DIFFERENCE BETWEEN SELF WORTH AND NET WORTH, WOMEN SUFFER TOO

In the twenty years I've worked with men, few have understood that self-worth and net worth are not connected. The majority feel they are one and the same, though, and the word feel is essential. A man who feels not just thinks that he is a failure because he hasn't achieved financial success, but feels that failure deep down in his male psyche, his male soul. That leaves men feeling depressed and frustrated. Most men won't achieve stellar financial success, and sadly, most will feel they've failed as men. Walking through life feeling like a failure based entirely on net worth is unimaginable. It should be unthinkable to every man.

Unless a man can distinguish between his self-worth and net worth, his life will be wasted feeling sorry for himself and everyone around him who he feels he's made suffer because of his lack of financial success. A man who buys into the notion that self-worth is all about net worth has bought into the worst possible lie about men. He has allowed people who have nothing to do with his life to define the nature and quality of his manhood.

Men frequently overlook the actual qualities that define selfworth. A husband who is considerate of his wife's hopes and dreams and supports her efforts to achieve them deserves a positive sense of self-worth. Money isn't involved in being a woman's cheerleader. Love and spirit have no financial basis. Ask any woman other than a Kardashian or Paris Hilton what qualities are most important in a man. A man who is intimately involved in raising his children, coaches their teams, goes to games, attends parent-teacher conferences, and teaches them good values, deserves to enjoy a strong sense of self-worth. Sure, his children might like lots of stuff that kids are bombarded with, but in the end, it's the love and attention a man gives his children that matter, not how much he can afford. Can't afford to take your kids to Disneyland? Take them camping instead and teach them about the real, natural world. It's about quality time and will allow you to connect with your kids far better than waiting in line for a ride that's over in a few minutes. A man who volunteers for community service, helping less fortunate folks, should feel good about his self-worth. Teaching people to read, tutoring disadvantaged children, helping with a community project, visiting elderly folks, working in a food bank, and many other activities define a man.

A man whose self-worth isn't in question is a man who nurtures friendships with other men and appreciates the value of authentic friendship. A man who can be there for a friend in trouble, or support a man whose life is upside down, is a man whose self-worth is intact.

There are several other ways a man can define his self-worth, but until most respond to the self-worth/net-worth paradigm in terms other than their checkbooks, net worth will remain the defining factor. That's entirely unacceptable to me and should be to every man. I won't give anyone the power to define my self-worth, and I won't feel I've done my part in the ongoing manhood debate until every man feels the same. Men should never allow anyone to define them in a manner that ignores who and what they are as men. Donald Trump has lots of money, but I doubt most women would find him a man they would like to be intimately involved with. Beyond his inherited money, and his net worth, there's little to redeem him as a man. A rich, loud-mouthed, fat guy with a bad comb-over and an inflated ego is a man who knows his self-worth is entirely dependent upon his net worth. The ego never determines self-worth. He is acting as a man does.

Men who work hard in their everyday lives to be good husbands, fathers, friends, and community volunteers have their self-worth in balance with their manhood. Their wives, children, and friends honor them for the manner they choose to live, not for their wallets. They will never be featured on the covers of magazines, but real men know that money isn't the basis for defining their self-worth or manhood. Selfworth depends upon knowing how to behave like a man, and women who want to be with a good man understand that.

CHAPTER 19

HOW TO IMPROVE YOUR SELFESTEEM AND SELF WORTH

My children constantly give me some great insights; this particular one came from my eldest, Sonnie. One day I noticed he went overboard with the ketchup on his dinner. When I asked him why all the ketchup, he said he didn't like the taste of the food and all this ketchup took the horrible taste away. Ketchup behaviors make life taste a little better while masking an underlying uncomfortable feeling or a feeling of emptiness.

Somebody asked me the other day, "Why do many people arrive midlife depressed or out of sorts?"

My response was that many of us arrive at midlife with a lot of unhappiness inside us without even realizing it, or we know it, but we don't want to face it up to it. To cover up the pain, we're likely to develop some severe addictions to feel better.

We get into immediate remedies - for example, medications, coffee, cigarettes, gossiping, alcohol, drugs, gambling, and sex. You might become a workaholic. Or you may stuff yourself with food.

Many things we do bring us instant pleasure but not always happy. Activities like these change how you feel fast, that's their appeal, but they're a terrible idea. At best, thcy will change how you think for few hours, but when the hit wears off, you feel more emptiness than you did before. Of course, there are countless positive ways of getting instant gratification as well. Something as simple as taking a shower after a long run, getting a massage, watching a funny movie, and shopping. We should all indulge in various forms of pleasure as they're essential to our well-being.

But remember, pleasure is different from happiness. Happiness is a feeling of fulfillment and profound joy, whereas pleasure is usually a form of instant gratification. This can be a challenge with excessive materialism. The more we feed it, the hungrier it becomes. Like eating your favorite chocolate, once eaten, you're soon looking for one more bite or the next cake. The craving doesn't subside. Contentment becomes elusive. So the passion for the next hit begins again, with the deep feelings of insecurity and anxiety.

Ketchup behaviors work in the short term, but in the long time does nothing more than reinforce an impoverished sense of self. Nothing external, no amount of cars, nice outfits, expensive holidays, glittery jewelry, or big houses can fill the hole of a poor self-image and low self-worth. Commonly this is known as having an 'inferiority complex.' It's a learned belief that says you're incomplete without attaining something outside of yourself. Self-worth comes from knowing who you are and what you stand for. When you have self-worth, you feel good about yourself; you respect yourself. Self-worth means knowing you are perfect just the way you are and accepting yourself completely. One of the reasons we fail to attract what we want is low self-worth. Self-worth is subjective and may or may not depend on your talents, skills, and achievements. If you feel that you are not worthy of having the life you want, then you will not manifest the life you want. Full stop!

It is not the skills, talents, and experience but a high sense of self-worth which manifests the life you want. So it is essential to improve your sense of self-worth to attract the life you desire.

One of the main reasons for low self-worth is excessive selfcriticism and the instant acceptance of criticism from others. If self-criticism is your problem, stop looking at yourself through your own eyes and start looking through the eyes of the people who love you. Many times, it is true that because of your obsessive self-criticism, you are blind to your positive qualities.

Sometimes it so happens that you start attracting the wealth, health, love, and success that you strongly desire, but your poor self-worth will quickly sabotage any success you are having. You've probably seen this happen to people who are suspicious of their lovers because of jealousy. At first, their intrinsic worthiness attracts the love of their life, but their low self-worth is not ready to accept this, and the worst part is they start suspecting it's their love's fault. Then, the thing they desire (their lover) is pushed away. And so the pattern repeats itself.

In midlife, we have to work hard at undoing the learned erroneous scripts formed in the first part of our life to find our expression of wisdom and truth.

Here are four things you can do to increase your self-worth:

1. Practice Forgiveness - Forgive yourself for past failures, mistakes, and disappointments. Forgiveness releases the intense feelings of hate and bitterness like poisons inside you. Correct what you can and move on!

2. Get your needs met - Learn what you need from others and how you react to situations. Strive to consistently find ways to meet your needs, and your self-worth will go up!

3. Respect yourself - Stop behaviors that make you feel ashamed, guilty, or unworthy. Eliminate all negative relationships with those who mistreat, disrespect, and leave you feeling crap!

4. Build on your strengths - Seek out and build on your muscles that you have not used. Find ways of using more of your innate strengths. Knowing that you have these strengths and can do well with them is a great confidence and selfworth builder.

Low self-worth is something we've learned, so it's also something we can unlearn. Make it a clear intention to love and accept yourself at all times. Working on your self-worth is one of the best things you can ever do for yourself, and before long, you'll notice you'll rely less on 'ketchup behaviors', and every aspect of your life will start looking better and better.

CHAPTER 20

SELF WORTH IS THE KEY TO POSITIVE SELF-ESTEEM

What would you say if I were to ask you today what your true value was? Would you answer through the eyes of another? Would your answer be the ghost voice of your mother, your ex, friends, enemies, or perhaps your coworkers? Where does the self worth come from? The fact is that self-esteem is external and self-worth is internal. These two are interwoven. What we feel internally radiates externally. What is your actual value? Your actual worth is what you feel your self-worth is; it is the beauty inside of you, the value you were born with. Self-worth shines from within to create the external feeling of self-esteem.

Many of us act as if self-esteem comes from what others think of us or how others perceive us. Sadly, many depend on the opinions of others as a measure of their self-esteem. For instance, if a person has a lot of friends, then they are perceived as having high self-esteem; in contrast, if a person has few friends, then the perception is there is low selfesteem. This is a false, inaccurate perception of what selfesteem is.

Self-esteem can only be measured and emitted from what we feel inside; it comes from what we perceive our self-worth to be. Many allow others to shatter their-worth, thus affecting self-esteem, but we must not let this happen. We must remember that no matter what others may say or think about us, we have the power to stay strong. We have the power to see ourselves for what we indeed are. We can be able to view ourselves the way the divine does. We must realize we are an image of the heavenly; as such, we are perfect in every way, even with all our imperfections. The great paradox is that those things we see as imperfections are simply perfect differences that make us exactly who we are, beautiful beings shining love through the projection of our self-worth. We must learn to love ourselves; in this love we learn to reclaim our self-worth and allow it to shine from the inside out as a reflection of our self-esteem.

Think about this, if I were to show you a - hundred-dollar bill and ask you what the value of it was? You would answer one hundred dollars. Perhaps the bill was torn in half and then taped back together. What would the value be then? One-hundred dollars, suitable? Then, if the bill had been stomped on, the importance of that bill would still be one hundred dollars.

Additionally, if I took the bill and yelled obscenities at it, would the deal still be one hundred dollars? Yes, of course, it would. The value of that one hundred-dollar bill is unwavering.

That is precisely how it should be for our self-worth. It should be unwavering. No matter what anyone says or writes about us, no matter what anyone does to us, we must believe in ourselves and keep our self-worth intact. Our self-worth is the key to our self-esteem and our power; it holds the answer to our true wealth. Through positive self-worth we will survive all the trials and tribulations of our life's journey. Our perception of our self-worth is precisely what we emit, which will be precisely what we will draw to ourselves in our life's path. Positive self-worth will draw favorable circumstances to us. Our task is to stay strong,, develop our self-worth, and claim our divine right to prosperity.

CHAPTER 21

FEELING WORTHLESS - HERE'S HOW TO BUILD UP YOUR SELFWORTH AND SELF RESPECT

I want to get to the heart of this topic because I firmly believe that there is a simple three-step approach that can cure feelings of worthlessness, even if you've felt crushed by those feelings for many years.

That's right: a cure.

It may not surprise you that doesn't feel very helpful is very common among women. You almost certainly know that. Feeling worthless is possibly the most obvious symptom of low self-esteem. But it's also one of the easiest to overcome. Let me provoke you for a moment by making a bold statement about worthlessness. You may want to reject it, but I urge you to hear me out on this point because I will show you how to prove this statement is true!

Feelings of worthlessness are entirely subjective. They are all in mind. They have no basis in reality. They do not constitute a problem that requires "fixing," and you can stop feeling worthless simply by opening your mind.

Fixing your self-esteem as a whole is not easy, but it is a reality for every woman.

OK, I know that some of you are now cross with me. You may even want to scream at me, "it's all very well for you to say that, but I've been feeling worthless all of my life, and I have no idea how to stop, and it's driving me CRAZY and, oh I'm so sick of being ME!"

Whether you're cross or not, I'd like you to think carefully about what I've got to say next. It's about how we might assess what something is worth.

What's the easiest thing to value?

How about a ten-dollar bill, in pristine condition, uncrumpled, never having changed hands?

It's worth 10 dollars, right? To you, to me, to anybody. Imagine sealing that newborn, crispy ten-dollar bill in a watertight container and dropping it in the middle of a deep lake. What's it worth now? Well, it's still got an intrinsic value of 10 dollars. Still, to hand it over to a storekeeper in exchange for some food, you'd have to rent a pretty sophisticated boat, some fancy detection equipment, and maybe a team of skilled drivers to get that box back. And that would cost you far more than ten dollars.

At the bottom of a lake, your perfect, crispy ten-dollar bill is worth less than nothing.

What's that got to do with you?

You had some intrinsic value when you were born. Everybody does. You could make the world a better place, bring joy and happiness to others, and experience a sense of emotional, spiritual, and physical fulfillment.

That was worth something. It still is. Because you still have the potential capacity to do jh,those things.

Our deepest fear is not that we are inadequate.

Our deepest fear is that we are powerful beyond measure.

It is our light, not our darkness that most frighten us.

- Marianne Williamson -

But what if you're an exception? What if your parents, the other kids at school, your ex-husband, or the rest of society has gradually knocked all of that potential worth out of you? Well, they haven't. I can be sure of that because it's impossible to take away a living person's capacity to add value to the world.

Only you can suppress that value. Only you can decide to hide away, feeling empty and alone. Only you can put yourself in the position of a ten-dollar bill at the bottom of a lake.

Do you see what power you have right there in your own hands?

No matter how tough your childhood, no matter how rotten your luck, you can CHOOSE to enrich the world every day simply by how you interact with others, how you make caring decisions and how you feel about yourself.

If you're feeling worthless right now, I'd like to ask you a question. What proactive steps have you been taking recently to overcome those feelings? Many women - when I put this question to them - answer with something like "um, well, nothing really because I feel stuck in a rut." Those women, all of them, are certainly not happy that they feel like that. But feeling like that is a habit that has become - almost paradoxically - a source of comfort to them. Why?

For one of two reasons:

1.   Feeling worthless is a safe option because it reduces the pain you suffer when things go wrong. If you already know that you're was no good and that no one will fall in love with you, give you a job, or even care enough to listen to you, then when a rejection wings its way towards you - which it certainly will because it happens to all of us - then you're better prepared than most. You can say: "Ah ha, you

can't ruin my life because I already knew this was going to happen; I already knew that you didn't love me/want me/value me!"

2.   Feeling worthless is an easy option; if you're worthless, there's no need to try to do well and succeed in the things that matter to you because there is simply no point. Also, if you act as if your opinions and desires are all worthless, then people leave you alone. If you say you have no remarkable skills or talents, then there is no need to apply them. Suppose you say you are a useless, hopeless nobody, then people will expect far less from you. And maybe you could get lots of sympathies and perhaps even another person (on a white horse in shining armor) coming to your rescue to sort your life out for you.

Deep down, all of us WANT to feel valued

But the harsh truth is we will feel valued only if we are willing to contribute something to the world around us. And whether we contribute anything or not is a choice. OUR choice.

A few of you might be annoyed with me at this point because you're still feeling worthless, but you do not agree that you are either choosing the safe, easy options or looking for a sympathy vote. If so, let's take a look at your logic.

Your annoyance can only be caused by the injustice of my suggestions you are choosing the "safe" or "easy" option.

You're saying to me, "Don't put me down. I'm not like that.

I AM WORTH MORE THAN THAT!"

That is exactly my point! Please remember, I am not the one doubting your self-worth; you are. All I'm doing is pointing out that if you're feeling worthless, then it simply means that you are not doing as well in the areas that matter to you, and therefore, you need to invest in your self-esteem. There are no exceptions: if you want to feel like a worthwhile human being, you have to work at it like everyone else and never give up on yourself.

It's up to you to acknowledge that all human beings are capable of adding value to society, including YOU. As an adult, there are no excuses for saying things like "I'm a worthless, stupid, lazy, ugly, useless, pathetic, helpless woman" because - as an adult - you now have the choice not to be any of these things.

All you have to do is acknowledge your actual value, accept it, and then commit to retain it and build upon it.

George Bernard Shaw once said:

"The people who get on in this world are those who get up and look for the circumstances they want, and if they can't find them, make them."

Woolly-thinking in the Self-esteem Movement

Remember that adage about the road to somewhere nasty being paved with good intentions? Here are just two examples.

•   The Self-esteem Movement has attempted to wrap us all in cotton wool for years now in the hope of protecting our precious self-esteem. It's the "self-esteem is our birthright" argument. Sadly, the only people who cling to this argument are people with low self-esteem who either have no idea how to improve matters or lack the will to do so. The view seduces them because it appears to hold out hope that "someone else" might somehow take responsibility for their lack of self-esteem and magically confer higher self-esteem upon them, like a court awarding compensation. This won't happen, and nor should it. If this argument has even slightly seduced you, try asking someone whom you consider to possess strong self-esteem whether she believes it was her birthright or whether she had to earn it for herself. You can guess what she'll tell you.

- The Self-esteem Movement seems to want us to believe that both self-esteem and self-worth are "binary" - that is, they exist in only one of two states like a light switch that can be on or off. You've either got self-esteem, or you haven't. Of course, this fits well with the first point, but it's not true. Your self-esteem is more like a mosaic - made up of lots of little pieces, some of which can be damaged or missing to the detriment of the whole. You can make minor improvements (baby steps, if you like) in one area or several areas simultaneously. Either way, the mosaic will become more defined, more robust, and more appealing.

The best path forward

Thankfully, I sense that the world is beginning to reject the "teachings" of the Self-esteem Movement. Their good intentions have not delivered the results that were hoped for. There is a far better path to tread, and it leads to somewhere meaningful. It's a path that anyone can follow if they want to. The signpost showing the way is this:

Self-esteem = doing well x feelgood factor

The truth is that NO ONE is worthless, but some people are worth more than others.

Of course,, some people are born with physical features that are generally considered more beautiful than the average person's. Other people are more intelligent, and some are more athletic, but none of this is as important as whether you make the most of who you are today and what you've got going for you right now. If you do this and keep doing this day in, and day-out for the rest of your life, I can guarantee that you will never feel worthless again. You'll be far too busy adding value here, there, and everywhere to stop and wallow in self-pity.

Right at the beginning of this article, I promised you a cure for worthlessness. Here it is, in thresteps:1.Acknowledge your real value by writing a list of your strengths, attributes, and the good things you do each day. If you've taken the Ultimate Self-esteem Test, then refer to your Self-esteem Profile, and the Self-help Programs recommended to you to remind yourself of your strengths and the areas you still need to work on. Accept this list as your starting point.

2.   Commit now to build your self-esteem and keep adding positive things to your life every day and find it within yourself to eliminate items from the opposing side. Do more smiling, share more kind thoughts and caring

emotions, be curious, optimistic, and courageous, work hard, and have fun. And reduce your time and energy in whingeing, moaning, or feeling sorry for yourself.

3.   Be your judge. You know yourself better than anyone, and now that you're an adult, it is up to you to decide your worth and to attempt to live up to realistic expectations of yourself. When I was living and working in Australia a few years ago, I heard for the first time the expression "tall poppy syndrome." It captures the notion that small-minded people often like to put down those who strive to do well because "tall poppies" make little weeds seem even smaller! Don't be afraid to be a tall poppy and enjoy the sun shining on you.

CHAPTER 22

SELF ESTEEM + SELF CONFIDENCE + SELF RESPECT = SELF WORTH! SELF = NET WORTH - WHAT ARE YOU WORTH?

Self-esteem is an internal sense of worth. It reflects inner confidence and self-respect, and it shines outwardly through the actions one takes.

The self-esteem that evolves on the inside is usually reflected on the outside. Your internal self-worth, which consists of your self-esteem, self-confidence, and selfrespect will become your external net worth. It is a matter of pride in who you are and the mentor you can be.

Compare an individual with solid self-esteem and high net worth to another with weak one and low net worth. What are the apparent differences? Does self-esteem play a significant role? Of course, it does. It is the essence of a personality.

Strong self-esteem produces confidence in oneself. Is it possible that positive self-esteem is the basis for a celebrated mindset? A mindset is a confident attitude that may draw from either a positive or negative self-esteem. Each perspective is the result of particular beliefs. What you believe to be true about yourself usually generates equivalent self-confidence and self-respect.

On a scale of 0 - 10 (low to high self-esteem), how would you rate your level of self-confidence and self-respect? Calculate the average level of the three senses of worth. The conclusion is your self-worth which ultimately determines your level of net worth as it pertains to business.

Please note there are ways to improve your self-confidence and, therefore, increase your level of self-worth. I believe we all came into this world at a level ten self-confidence. We were equal human beings regardless of race, religion, color, nationality, sex, title, or role.

However, our exposure to the outside world - family, religion, education, politics, etc. permits outside influences to overshadow our true self-confidence. We have fashioned our fears, limitations, and boundaries on what we experience, see, and hear.

Over time, our perceptions have been altered. Our selfesteem is diminished, and our self-worth suddenly has limitations.

We are innovative, educated adults and should be able to distinguish between fact and fiction. We need to go back and review our values as it relates to self-esteem. We need to remove some of the baggage that has been holding us back, lowering our self-esteem, self-confidence, and self-respect. We need to boost our self-confidence by acknowledging our worth and managing our emotions. Our self-confidence portrays our values and affects the choices we make. By changing our internal thinking, we can reclaim our selfesteem, self-confidence, and self-respect and strive for a level ten self-esteem as our standard. This is a level of selfesteem from which to begin, not end.

It is known that if we don't believe in ourselves, no one else will either. How we feel about ourselves, and our selfesteem, is reflected in our daily conversations, our body language, and abilities. We are responsible for our destiny; anything is possible with high quality self-esteem. There are ways to boost your self-confidence. Begin by setting attainable goals for yourself. Make your dreams a reality. Accept support and encouragement from others.

Learn from your mistakes.

It won't take long before your self-esteem is back to ten or more. Realistically, self-respect is also the difference between success and failure. We all want success, and therefore, we must do whatever it takes to boost our selfesteem daily.

What results are you looking for? What actions must you take? What type of self-confidence do you need to experience self-worth?

It would help if you believed in yourself - the most critical person in the world. You are the all-inclusive package of self-esteem, self-confidence, and self-respect. All three attributes equal your self-worth, and in turn, your self-worth will translate externally into your net worth.

CHAPTER 23

THINGS THAT DON'T DETERMINE YOUR SELF-WORTH

❖ Your To-Do List

Crossing off items on your to-do list is a satisfying feeling, but you can't let the number of things you crossed off your list (or the number of things you don't) control your worth. "While it's normal to feel proud of your accomplishments, basing your entire self-worth on your achievement is like building a house on an unsteady foundation," Morin writes. "You'll need to experience constant success to feel good about yourself—and that means you'll likely avoid doing things where you could fail."

❖ Your Job

No matter the type of job you have or how much you love (or hate) it, your job doesn't define who you are as a person.

❖ Your Social Media Following

So what if you don't have a million Insta followers or

Twitter retweets? In this digital world, it can feel like that number determines your value, but you're more complex than anyone can see on a screen.

❖ Your Age

Speaking of numbers, your age is just a number. Some people may say you're too young or too old, but that's just who you are now, so just be.

❖ Your Appearance

If you want to change your look, do it for yourself. But know that your physical appearance shouldn't define how worthy you are. "A beautiful body or a handsome face won't last forever," Morin writes. "Hair loss, wrinkles, and a middleage spread can feel catastrophic for someone whose selfworth depends on their physical appearance."

❖ Other People

I'm guilty of comparing myself to others who have the same job title and my age. But I've learned I must manifest in my lane—and so should you.

Manifest in your lane.

You do you. Let them do them. Sometimes others may pass you on this road called life, and that's OK. We're all traveling at different speeds.

❖ How Far You Can Run

Tell yourself you'll run a mile and then beat yourself up when you couldn't? It happens, but know that your worth comes from trying at all, not how quickly you crush a goal.

❖ Your Grades

Maybe tests freak you out, or school is just tough. Your grades don't determine your intelligence and don't measure things like your dedication and integrity.

❖ The Number of Friends You Have

The more friends, the merrier. Sometimes. But whether you have a ton of friends or just a couple, what matters is how you treat one another and if you can turn to them in times of need.

❖ Your Relationship Status

Single shingle. It doesn't mean you're not worthy of love or of being loved—you're doing you and focusing on loving yourself.

❖ The Money (or Lack Thereof) in the Bank

Whether you're a billionaire or don't have much in your wallet, the amount of money you have or are making doesn't define your worth. "Going deep into debt to create a façade of wealth backfires in the end because while goods and services have monetary value, they don't reflect your value as a human being," Morin writes.

❖ Your Likes

I'm not talking about Facebook likes, but your likes, such as your taste in music or movies. Like what you want, whether it may be considered "high art" or "low art."

CONCLUSION

Your worth is entirely up to you. You are worthy because you say you're respected and because you believe it. Look within, and trust that you are enough.

All in all, a person will gain self-confidence from their own experience and decision. No one speech or conversation can bring an overnight change. It is a gradual but constant process we must all participate in. It will take time, but once you achieve it, nothing can stop you from conquering every height.